A Quest for Good Manners

Story by
Karin Lefranc

Pictures by
Hannah Neale

BELUGA PRESS

SIMSBURY · CONNECTICUT

Sparkler slurped his soup and wiped his enormous mouth with his enormous paw. "More!" he roared.

"Yes, more!" shouted Princess Rosalind. She banged her fist on the table, spilling her milk.

"That is enough from both of you. Rosalind, you will learn to behave, as will that rude dragon of yours," the queen declared.

Rosalind shoved a big spoonful of mashed potatoes into her mouth. "But, Mom, princesses don't need manners, and Sparkler doesn't know any better. He is just a dragon," she said, spluttering potato bits everywhere.

"Princesses and dragons—and everyone in between—need to learn how to behave," said the queen.

"What's the big deal with manners anyway?" muttered Rosalind, flicking a pea at Sparkler. "It's just a bunch of boring rules."

Sparkler nodded and snapped up the flying pea. Then he burped a long spray of flames, just like a sparkler.

"I cannot enjoy my dinner with you two slurping and burping. You have three days to find Good Manners, or I will banish that dragon!" said the queen as she stormed out of the royal dining room.

"Oh, pickle juice, what are we going to do now?" Rosalind moaned, playing with her vegetables. "We must find Percival. If anyone can help us, that old wizard can."

› › ›

The next day, after a very messy breakfast, Rosalind wiped her eggy hands on Sparkler's scaly back. Then she ducked her head as they flew out the dining room window to find Percival.

"Good morning, Princess Rosalind. How are you today?" asked Percival politely.

"Terrible," she replied, without even a nice thank you for asking or a pleasant good morning. "Mom won't let me keep Sparkler until we both find Good Manners, and we've only got two days left."

"It sounds like you are on a quest," said Percival.

"What's a quest?" asked Rosalind.

"It's a special journey to find something very important," Percival explained. "If you are able to pull the golden fork from that rock, it will guide you in your journey."

Rosalind pulled and pulled until her hands were red and sore. "I just can't do it," she cried.

"It's not a matter of strength, Rosalind, but how you hold the fork," Percival hinted.

Rosalind wrapped her fingers gently around the fork. The rock creaked and groaned. Suddenly, the rubies on the handle sparkled brightly, and the fork slid out.

"Well done, you have passed your first challenge," said Percival. "Remember—never grab your fork with a fist."

Waving good-bye to the wizard, Rosalind and Sparkler soared into the clouds, flying over oceans and mountains and fields of wheat and corn. Suddenly, the fork jerked, pointing down to a glassy lake.

Bump, boing, BANG! "When will you learn to land smoothly?" demanded Rosalind. "Good thing I am really hot because I think we are supposed to swim across." Rosalind splashed through the cool water, and Sparkler followed, puffing smoke and flames with each stroke.

When they reached the other side, a steep ledge prevented them from climbing onto shore.

"Can I help you?" asked a fairy with purple wings.

"Obviously, we need help," cried Rosalind.

The fairy turned her back, flapping her wings slowly. "You forgot the magic word that makes men, women, children— and fairies—want to help you."

Rosalind spluttered, "Oh, I get it. Please, will you help us?"

"Why, certainly," said the fairy, easily lifting Rosalind and Sparkler out of the water. The fairy folded her arms across her chest. "Now what do you say?"

"Thank you. Thank you so much for helping us," they both said quickly.

"Good," said the fairy. "You're welcome. Always remember to say please, thank you, and you're welcome, as these simple words show that you care about people and fairies."

"I am sorry we were so rude to you before," said Rosalind. At once the rubies in the fork lit up.

"Well done, Rosalind. You have passed your second challenge," said the fairy. "Those three magic words can right many wrongs."

The fork turned to point north. Waving good-bye to the fairy, they flew over oceans and mountains and fields of wheat and corn until they saw the craggy icebergs of Icetopia.

This time Sparkler's landing turned into a long slide that finally stopped at the entrance of a glittering ice castle.

A tall, elegant woman opened the door. "Welcome to my home. My name is Lady Grace," she said. "Please join me for lunch."

"Thank you very much," said Rosalind, her stomach rumbling. "We are on a quest for Good Manners."

"Yes, I know. The north winds have carried news of your arrival," said Lady Grace. "Today we will learn good table manners."

They sat down at a magnificent table. "First, place your napkins in your laps," said Lady Grace. "Guard them well, as they will save you from many embarrassing moments."

Carefully watching Lady Grace, Rosalind took small bites and chewed with her mouth closed. Sparkler even managed to keep his scaly elbows off the table.

The food was delicious until Lady Grace offered them something green and slimy. "Would you like some Icetopia seaweed?"

"No, thank you, Lady Grace," replied Rosalind politely.

Even Sparkler, who was definitely not a picky eater, looked nervously at the platter and stammered, "Nnno—thank you—Lady Grace."

"Well done, you have answered well," replied Lady Grace.

Suddenly, they heard a *tap*, *tap*, *tap* at the door. Lady Grace nodded to Rosalind and Sparkler to open the door. A ragged boy not much older than Rosalind stood there. "May I have a glass of water? I am surrounded by ice but no fresh water." He laughed nervously.

"This is not our castle," Sparkler said, "but I am sure Lady Grace will give you some water."

"Better yet, we'll ask if you can join us for dinner," Rosalind added.

The boy's face lit up, and so did the magic fork. "Thank you! Many days have passed since my last meal."

"Well done, Rosalind and Sparkler, you have passed the final challenge," said Lady Grace. "The secret to Good Manners is showing kindness and consideration to others."

"Hurray!" Sparkler roared. "Now can we go home, Rosalind?"

"Yes, Sparkler, we can go home as soon as we finish dinner and thank Lady Grace," Rosalind replied.

With their bellies full, they sailed over oceans, mountains, and fields of wheat and corn. When, at last, they saw their castle, Sparkler landed gracefully next to the queen's rose garden.

"Just in time for dinner," the queen said. "Would you like to join us, Sparkler?"

"Yes, please, your majesty, Sparkler's always ready for food!"

Taking Rosalind's arm, he escorted her into the royal dining room, where they enjoyed a feast fit for a queen—and a princess, and a dragon.

Marveling at their newfound Good Manners, the queen said, "You have succeeded in your quest. Sparkler, you may dine with us every day. Just no flames indoors, please."

"Thank you," cried Rosalind. "You're the best queen—and mom—in the whole world!"

For Madeleine, Beatrice, Josephine and Eric—who have taught me
as much about good manners as I have taught them

—K.L.

For Christine

—H.N.

Editing by Nancy Day
Book Design by Fiona Raven

Manufactured by Friesens Corporation
in Altona, Canada
First Printing January 2011
Job # 62225

Published by Beluga Press
Simsbury, CT
info@belugapress.com
www.BelugaPress.com

For information, visit
www.AQuestForGoodManners.com

First Published in June 2011

Library of Congress Control Number 2010918054

Publisher's Cataloging-in-Publication Data
(Prepared by The Donohue Group, Inc.)
Lefranc, Karin.
    A quest for good manners / by Karin Lefranc ;
illustrated by Hannah Neale.
    p. : col. ill. ; cm.
Summary: A princess and her dragon go on a quest for good
manners so they won't be banned from the Queen's table.
Interest age level: 003–007.
ISBN 978-0-9830459-0-8
1. Etiquette for children and teenagers—Juvenile fiction.
2. Princesses—Juvenile fiction. 3. Dragons—Juvenile fiction.
4. Etiquette—Fiction. 5. Behavior—Fiction. 6. Princesses—
Fiction. 7. Dragons—Fiction. I. Neale, Hannah, 1981-
II. Title.
PZ7.L44 Q84 2011
[Fic]   2010918054

⟩ ⟩ ⟩

Distributed by Emerald Book Company
For ordering information or special discounts for bulk purchases,
please contact Emerald Book Company at
PO Box 91869, Austin, TX 78709
(512) 891-6100